Grant Allen, J. Illingworth Kay

The Lower Slopes

Reminiscences of Excursions Round the Base of Helicon

Grant Allen, J. Illingworth Kay

The Lower Slopes
Reminiscences of Excursions Round the Base of Helicon

ISBN/EAN: 9783337190651

Printed in Europe, USA, Canada, Australia, Japan

Cover: Foto ©Andreas Hilbeck / pixelio.de

More available books at **www.hansebooks.com**

THE·LOWER·SLOPES

REMINISCENCES OF
EXCURSIONS ROUND THE
BASE OF HELICON, UNDER-
-TAKEN FOR THE MOST PART
IN EARLY MANHOOD: BY
GRANT ALLEN.

LONDON: ELKIN MATHEWS
& JOHN LANE   AT THE SIGN OF
THE BODLEY HEAD.   1894.
CHICAGO: STONE & KIMBALL

CONTENTS

IN MAGDALEN TOWER

My brain is weary and my eyes are aching
   With poring over long on Plato's text;
I'll make this silent hour my own, forsaking
   The buried lore with which my soul is vexed.
The breeze without blows kindlier and moister;
   I'll fling the mullioned window open wide
That looks athwart the solemn court and cloister,
   To view the world outside.

Each dome and spire from east to west arises
   An island from the rolling sea of mist
That fills with shadowy waves the vale of Isis,
   All save the imperial city's queenly crest.
Above, the chilly moonbeams of October
   Wrap round her sleeping form a gilded shroud:
Below, the fleecy sheets of vapour robe her
   In folds of silver cloud.

A

The blood-red creeper on the pale grey turret
    Shows purple in the dim recess of night,
Save when the short-lived autumn breezes stir it,
    Flashing a gleam of crimson on my sight.
And drooping ivy sprays that twist and dangle
    Around the gloomy gurgoyles' mouldering
        mass
Shed ghostly shadows on the dark quadrangle,
    Across the moonlit grass.

Hard by, the clear-cut pinnacles of Merton
    Rise black against the wan abyss on high ;
The far Cathedral steeple looms uncertain
    Through intervening depths of hazy sky :
High in the tapering belfry of St. Mary's
    The solemn clock knells out the stroke of
        three,
And fills with floating sound and weird vagaries
    The misty middle sea.

These dreamy reveries of Plato mingle
    With shapeless cloud and voices of vague bells
To bid each vein through all my body tingle,
    And stir my brain through all its throbbing cells.
The city's form melts like the fitful vapour,
    Till these her solid walls of massive stone,
Unreal as the fleecy robes that drape her,
    Fade, and I stand alone.

I know not if she be or if she be not ;
  I only know I am, and nought beside :
I gaze abroad with timid eyes and see not
  Beyond the mist by which my sight is tied.
The things I see and hear and feel around me
  Merge in the inner consciousness of thought :
Yet like an iron chain their limits bound me
  With bands myself have wrought.

Is sentient life,—set passive in the middle
  Of fleeting sights and sounds, of joy and pain,
Yearning yet impotent, an awful riddle
  Whose hidden end we seek to solve in vain : —
Is life, so strangely placed, a wanton creature
  Of calm design that heeds not human cares,
Or bastard offspring of unconscious nature
  Begotten unawares ?

When chaos slowly set to sun or planet
  And molten masses hardened into earth,
When primal force wrought out on sea and granite
  The wondrous miracle of living birth,
Did mightier Mind, in clouds of glory hidden,
  Breathe power through its limbs to speak and
    know,
Or sentience spring spontaneous and unbidden,
  With feeble steps and slow ?

Are sense and thought but parasites of being?
    Did nature mould our limbs to act and move,
But some strange chance endow our eyes with
      seeing,
    Our nerves with feeling and our hearts with love?
Since all alone we stand, alone discerning
    Sorrow from joy, self from the things without:
While blind fate tramples on our spirit's yearning
    And fills our souls with doubt.

This very tree, whose life is our life's sister,
    We know not if the ichor in her veins
Thrill with fierce joy when April dews have kissed
      her,
    Or shrink in anguish from October rains.
We search the mighty world above and under,
    Yet nowhere find the soul we fain would find,
Speech in the hollow rumbling of the thunder,
    Words in the whispering wind.

We yearn for brotherhood with lake and mountain;
    Our conscious soul seeks conscious sympathy,
Nymphs in the coppice, Naiads in the fountain,
    Gods on the craggy height and roaring sea.
We find but soulless sequences of matter,
    Fact linked to fact by adamantine rods,
Eternal bonds of former sense and latter,
    Dead laws for living Gods.

They care not any whit for pain or pleasure
   That seem to men the sum and end of all :
Dumb force and barren number are their measure ;
   What can be, shall be, though the great world
      fall.
They take no heed of man or man's deserving,
   Reck not what happy lives they make or mar,
Work out their fatal will, unswerved, unswerving,
   And know not that they are.

Can lifeless law beget on senseless matter
   The fuller life of self-reflecting thought?
Or may the pregnant soul itself but scatter
   These myriad fancies through a world of nought?
Are all these outer shapes a vain illusion
   (As in deep tones our clearest prophet sings),
And mind alone, set free from vague confusion,
   The inmost core of things ?

The city lies below me, wrapped in slumber ;
   Mute and unmoved in all her streets she lies :
Mid rapid thoughts that throng me without
      number
   Flashes the image of an old surmise :
Her hopes and fears and griefs are all suspended ;
   Ten thousand souls throughout her precincts
      take
Sleep, in whose bosom life and death are blended,
   And I alone awake.

Am I alone the solitary centre
　　Of all the seeming universe around,
With mocking senses through whose portals enter
　　Unmeaning fantasies of sight and sound?
Are all the countless minds wherewith I people
　　The empty forms that float before my eyes
Vain as the cloud that girds the distant steeple
　　With snowy canopies?

Yet though the world be but myself unfolded,
　　Soul bent again on soul in mystic play,
No less each sense and thought and act is moulded,
　　By dead necessities I may not sway.
Some mightier power against my will can move
　　me,
　　Some potent nothing force and overawe;
Though I be all that is, I feel above me
　　The godhead of blind law.

I seem a passive consciousness of passion
　　Poised in the boundless vault of empty space;
A mirror for strange shapes of alien fashion
　　That come and go before my lonely face.
My soul that reigns the mistress of creation,
　　That grasps within herself the sum of things,
Wears round her feet the gyves of limitation,
　　And fetters bind her wings.

The sense I fain would feel I cannot summon;
 The sense I fain would shirk I cannot shun:
I know the measured sequence that they come in;
 I may not change the grooves wherein they
 run.
I know not if they be but phantom faces
 Whose being is but seeming, seen awry:
They pass, I know not how, and leave no traces;
 They come I know not why.

My inmost hope, my deepest aspiration,
 Each quiver of my brain, each breath I draw,
Fear curdling up the blood, love's wild pulsation,
 Work surely out the inevitable law:
The will herself that pants for freedom, flouting
 Its soulless despotism, yet works it out:
Ay, even though I doubt, my very doubting
 Fulfils the law I doubt.

So, dimly cloaked in infinite disguises,
 The hopes I seem to grasp again dissolve,
And through their vacant images arises
 The central problem that I may not solve;
Till, like this fading creeper's blighted blossom,
 My life too fade before some wintry breath,
And sink at last upon the peaceful bosom
 Of all-embracing death.

But now that far and wide the pale horizon,
   Faint grey to eastward, darker on the west,
Lights up the misty sphere its border lies on,
   My weary brain has need of gentle rest.
The growing haze of sunrise gives me warning
   To check these wayward thoughts that dive too
     deep.
Perchance a little light will come with morning,
   Perchance I shall but sleep.

A BALLADE OF EVOLUTION

In the mud of the Cambrian main
　　Did our earliest ancestor dive :
From a shapeless albuminous grain
　　We mortals our being derive.
He could split himself up into five,
　　Or roll himself round like a ball ;
For the fittest will always survive,
　　While the weakliest go to the wall.

As an active ascidian again
　　Fresh forms he began to contrive,
Till he grew to a fish with a brain,
　　And brought forth a mammal alive.
With his rivals he next had to strive
　　To woo him a mate and a thrall ;
So the handsomest managed to wive,
　　While the ugliest went to the wall.

At length as an ape he was fain
　　The nuts of the forest to rive,
Till he took to the low-lying plain,
　　And proceeded his fellows to knive.

Thus did cannibal men first arrive
One another to swallow and maul :
And the strongest continued to thrive,
While the weakliest went to the wall.

ENVOY

Prince, in our civilised hive,
Now money 's the measure of all ;
And the wealthy in coaches can drive,
While the needier go to the wall.

THE RETURN OF APHRODITE

Deep in Cythera a cave,
   Pealing a thunderous pæan,
Roars, as the shivering wave
   Whitens the purple Ægean :
There to astonish the globe,
   Terrible, beautiful, mighty,
Clad with desire as a robe,
   Rose Aphrodite.

Never again upon earth
   Like her arose any other ;
Got without labour or birth,
   Sprung without father or mother :
Zeus, from his aery home,
   Seeing the roseate water
Lift her aloft on its foam,
   Hailed her his daughter.

Sweet was her shape, and is now ;
   Sweeter the breath of her kisses ;
Delicate ivory brow ;
   Wealth of ambrosial tresses ;

Mouth that no favour denies ;
  Cheek that no ardour abashes ;
Languishing eyelids and eyes,
  Languishing lashes.

Then, as her luminous face
  Shone like the ocean that bore her,
Every nation and race
  Worshipped her, falling before her ;
Chaplets they culled for her fane,
  Fairer than any can cull us ;
Greece gave her Sappho's refrain,
  Rome her Catullus.

Soft was the sound of their lyre,
  Luscious their lay without cloying,
Till, as a billow of fire,
  Crushing, consuming, destroying,
Wasting her wines in their spleen,
  Spilling her costly cosmetics,
Swept the implacable, lean
  Horde of ascetics.

Darkness they spread over earth,
  Sorrow and fasting of faces ;
Mute was the music of mirth,
  Hushed was the chorus of Graces ;

Back to the womb of the wave,
  Terrible, beautiful, mighty,
Back with the boons that she gave
  Sank Aphrodite.

Down the abysses of time
  Rolled the unchangeable ages,
Reft of the glory of rhyme
  Graven in passionate pages ;
Sad was the measure, and cold,
  Dead to the language of kisses ;
Sadly the centuries rolled
  Down the abysses.

Now in the ends of the earth
  Tenderer singers and sweeter,
Smit with a ravening dearth,
  Cry on the goddess and greet her ;
Cry with their rapturous eyes
  Flashing the fire of emotion ;
Call her again to arise
  Fresh from the ocean.

Hot as of old are their songs,
  Breathing of odorous tresses,
Murmur of amorous tongues,
  Ardour of fervid caresses ;

Trilled with a tremulous mouth
  Into the ear of the comer,
Warm as the breath of the South,
  Soft as the Summer.

Under the depth of the wave,
  Hearing their passionate numbers,
Piercing her innermost cave,
  Waken her out of her slumbers,
Soothed with the sound of their strain,
  Beautiful, merciful, mighty,
Back to the nations again
  Comes Aphrodite.

SUNDAY AT BRAEMAR

ALONE amid the solemn heathy desert
  Whose bleak brown sides o'erhang Braemar,
I sit, this misty Scottish August Sabbath,
  High up the spurs of Lochnagar.

Above, fierce swirls of moaning autumn weather
  Drive on thin wreaths of vaporous cloud;
While, hanging low, the blight that dims the back-
    ground
  Spreads o'er heaven's face its sullen shroud.

Beneath me heaves afar one solid ocean,
  Wave after wave of moor and ben,
Flung seething up in granite-crested billow,
  Or sunk in troughs of sweeping glen.

No laughing eye of silver-rippled lakelet,
  But black expanse of peaty loch,
Whose moody depths unstirred obscurely mirror
  Fantastic forms of gaunt grey rock.

No golden croft or grassy-tedded homestead ;
　No close-cropped lawn of ruddled sheep ;
But holt and hurst where roam high-antlered
　　faces,
　And purple moors where grey grouse creep.

While here and there some low-browed, turf-built
　　shieling
　Peeps out through friths of fir or birk,
Where frowns, austere, elect, the shingled
　　steeple
　That tops some sombre granite kirk.

But leagues between, a vagrant sunbeam flashes
　On palace wall or castled pride,
Thronged with gay-kilted crowds whose lairdly
　　pleasures
　Spread Libyan desert far and wide.

Who thrust across wild waves of western ocean
　Disacred remnants of great clans ;
Who gave to fir and whins and forest roamers
　The generous haughs that once were man's.

As dazed I scan this weary waste of heather,
　And desolate haunts of bird or deer,
And lonely homes of selfish Saxon splendour,
　A southern cry rings in my ear.

A cry that, bursting from ten thousand bosoms,
  Awoke from midnight into noon
Marseille, Bordeaux, Saint Étienne, Lyon, Paris,
  With lips that shrieked ' Vive la Commune!'

My thirsty vision pants for sunlit waters,
  And luscious glebe of vine-clad lands,
And chanted psalms of universal freedom,
  And sacred grasp of brotherly hands :

Pants to behold the ruddy Highland ranger,
  With fair-cheeked sons of English soil,
Linked to the sunburnt throng of southern cities
  In one vast commonwealth of toil :

Banded to break the pride of hoarded treasure,
  Or insolent boast of lordly birth :
To fling the equal boon of freeborn manhood
  Through all the spreading skirts of earth :

No longer with the red right hand of slaughter,
  Nor eyes made drunk with blood and wine ;
But sober sweat of brows whose slow endeavour
  Piles surely up the grand design :

Not eager to forestall in raw impatience
  The lagging wheels of distant years,
But planning well a deep-set revolution,
  Unstained by blot of blood or tears.

B

Till once again that holy cry re-echo
    From mightier crowds and louder still,
Through ocean-sundered streets, with happier
    auspice
    Of undivided human will:

And once again this dreary Scottish landscape
    With golden dimples smile afar,
Spreading the nobler wealth of happy harvests
    High up the slopes of Lochnagar:

While, side by side, the men of many nations
    Blend in one boundless league and free,
As Thames and Seine, St. Lawrence, Nile, and
    Ganges
    Mingle in one illimitable sea.

THE FIRST IDEALIST

A JELLY-FISH swam in a tropical sea,
And he said, 'This world it consists of Me :
There's nothing above and nothing below
That a jelly-fish ever can possibly know
(Since we've got no sight, or hearing, or smell),
Beyond what our single sense can tell.
Now, all that I learn from the sense of touch
Is the fact of my feelings, viewed as such.
But to think they have any external cause
Is an inference clean against logical laws.
Again, to suppose, as I've hitherto done,
There are other jelly-fish under the sun,
Is a pure assumption that can't be backed
By a jot of proof or a single fact.
In short, like Hume, I very much doubt
If there's anything else at all without.
So I come at last to the plain conclusion,
When the subject is fairly set free from confusion,

That the universe simply centres in Me,
And if *I* were not, then nothing would be.'

That minute, a shark, who was strolling by,
Just gulped him down, in the twink of an eye;
And he died, with a few convulsive twists.

But, somehow, the universe still exists.

FOR AMY LEVY'S URN

THIS bitter age that pits our maids with men
    Wore out her woman's heart before its time :
            Too wan and pale,
            She strove to scale
    The icy peaks of unimagined rhyme.
There, worlds broke sunless on her frighted ken ;
    The mountain air struck chill on her frail breath :
Fainting she fell, all weary with her climb,
    And kissed the soft, sweet lips of pitying death.

A PRAYER

A CROWNED Caprice is god of this world ;
On his stony breast are his white wings furled.
No ear to listen, no eye to see,
No heart to feel for a man hath he.

But his pitiless arm is swift to smite ;
And his mute lips utter one word of might,
Mid the clash of gentler souls and rougher,
' Wrong must thou do, or wrong must suffer.'

Then grant, oh dumb blind god, at least that we
Rather the sufferers than the doers be.

IN CORAL LAND

A TINY fay
Deep nestling lay
In a purple bay
  Unruffled
On whose crystal floor
The distant roar
From the surf-bound shore
  Was muffled.

With his fairy wife
He passed his life
Undimmed by strife
  Or quarrel ;
And the live-long day
They would merrily play
Through a labyrinth gay
  With coral.

They loved to dwell
In a pearly shell,
And to deck their cell
   With amber :
Or amid the caves
That the ripplet laves
And the beryl paves
   To clamber.

By the limpet's home
And the vaulted dome
Where the starfish roam
   They 'd linger ;
In the mackerel's jaw
And the lobster's claw
They 'd push and withdraw
   A finger.

And queer little things
With filmy wings
And floating strings
   To guide them,
Of softest mould,
In swarms untold,
Tumbled and rolled
   Beside them.

On a darting shrimp
Our frolicsome imp
With bridle of gimp
  Would gambol ;
Or astride on the back
Of a sea-horse black
(As a gentleman's hack)
  He 'd amble.

Of emerald green
And sapphire's sheen
He made his queen
  A tiar ;
And the merry two
Their whole life through
Were as happy as you
  And I are.

But if you say
You think this lay
Of the tiny fay
  Too silly,
Let it have such praise
As my eye betrays
To your own sweet gaze,
  My Millie !

For a man, he tries,
And he toils and sighs,
To be mighty wise
    And witty ;
But a dear little dame
Has enough of fame
If she wins the name
    Of pretty.

AN ANSWER

'But there! no man ever loved any woman well enough to love her only.'—*Extract from a Letter.*

THE shallow pool, content to woo the charms
   Of one coy mead, gapes dry in August days :
The mightiest ocean winds enamoured arms
   Round countless capes in deep caressing bays.

I hold that heart full poor that owns its boast
   To throb in tune with but one throbbing breast.
Who numbers many friends, loves friendship most ;
   Who numbers many loves, loves each love best.

FOR A SPECIAL OCCASION

(BOULGE CHURCHYARD, OCT. 5, 1893)

HERE, on Fitzgerald's grave, from Omar's tomb,
To lay fit tribute pilgrim singers flock.
Long with a double fragrance let it bloom,
This rose of Iran on an English stock.

THE NEW POETRY

TO RICHARD LE GALLIENNE

My name is Aphrodite, and my home
   Men decked of old in flowery fanes of Greece :
   All other gods were born, died, and have peace :
I only spring eternal from the foam ;
   I still am queen ; my reign shall never cease.

One other was not born, nor yet has died ;
   Pallas, who leapt all armed from Zeus's head
   (Pallas, my foe, a virgin never wed) ;
We twain sprang not from any mother's side ;
   Therefore we live, though other gods be dead.

We twain divide the hearts and loves of men ;
   For some are strong and cold and heed me not ;
   And softer some have passionate hearts and hot.
But women cleave to me : where she wins ten,
   A thousand lovesome maids fall to my lot.

We twain have war whose term is never said
    For all the hearts of men and all their loves.
    My throat is warm ; it thrills like my own doves';
And soft as summer breezes do I tread :
    Her throat is cold, and like strong winds she
      moves.

Mine are the gentle lives that yearn to stray,
    Heart locked in heart, red lips to pale lips
      pressed,
    Together down smooth paths of wedded rest,
Till crimson memories of departing day
    Swathe in voluptuous tints the gorgeous West.

Hers are the sphere-like souls whose boundless
      view
    Can spy the subtle motions of the brain,
    Unfold entangled webs of joy and pain,
Or track through varying moods the Good and
      True.
    Them woo I with my amorous lures in vain.

Mine are the hands that limn with cunning stains
    The ineffable meekness of Madonna's face ;
    That quicken marble limbs to effluent grace :
Mine are the throats that trill forth rippling
      strains
    Of liquid treble, or thunderous floods of bass.

Hers are the piercing orbs whose keener power
   Sights starry isles that stud the nebulous main :
   Hers are such hands as range the infinite train
Of insect, beast, and bird, of fern and flower.
   Them too with dangled lures I woo in vain.

But votaries dearer to her heart than these—
   Fingers that know the dainty skill to twine
   Blossoms of thought in garlands for her shrine—
Sweet poets, who were once her devotees,
   Have I enticed away, and *they* are mine.

UT FLOS IN SEPTIS

As a lily that lurks half-hid in the innermost nook
  of a garden,
Whose sinews the showers feed, and the bountiful
  breezes harden :
And never a heifer there can crop it close with the
  grasses ;
And never a murderous share can crush it to earth
  as it passes ;
But thick with its odorous sighs the wings of the
  wind are laden,
And it stands a coveted prize for many a lad and
  maiden :

Until in a luckless day some boy in that innermost
  bower
Has gathered in wanton play the snow-white
  virginal flower ;
And its stem that the showers fed fades fast, and
  its sweet bells languish,
And it hangs its beautiful head in the infinite
  weight of its anguish ;

And its leaves that were once so fair droop down-
    ward, heavily laden,
And never a lad would care for it now, nor ever
    a maiden :

Such, in the innocent days of her snow-white
    virginal season,
Is the maiden whom love betrays ere love has
    spoken his treason :
But when one feverish night has fathered a
    penitent morrow,
The bloom of her brief delight fades fast into
    infinite sorrow ;
And her eye, that was blithe with joy, with tears
    brims, bitterly laden,
For now nor ever a boy will love her, nor ever a
    maiden.

ONLY AN INSECT

I

On the crimson cloth
  Of my study desk
A lustrous moth
  Poised statuesque.
Of a waxen mould
  Were its light limbs shaped,
And in scales of gold
  Its body was draped :
While its luminous wings
  Were netted and veined
With silvery strings,
  Or golden grained,
Through whose filmy maze
  In tremulous flight
Danced quivering rays
  Of the gladsome light.

II

On the desk hard by
  A taper burned,
Towards which the eye
  Of the insect turned.
In its vague little mind
  A faint desire
Rose, undefined,
  For the beautiful fire.
Lightly it spread
  Each silken van ;
Then away it sped
  For a moment's span.
And a strange delight
  Lured on its course
With resistless might
  Towards the central source :
And it followed the spell
  Through an eddying maze,
Till it fluttered and fell
  In the deadly blaze.

III

Dazzled and stunned
  By the scalding pain,
One moment it swooned,
  Then rose again ;

And again the fire
    Drew it on with its charms
To a living pyre
    In its awful arms ;
And now it lies
    On the table here
Before my eyes
    Shrivelled and sere.

IV

As I sit and muse
    On its fiery fate,
What themes abstruse
    Might I meditate !
For the pangs that thrilled
    Through that martyred frame
As its veins were filled
    With the scorching flame,
A riddle enclose
    That, living or dead,
In rhyme or in prose,
    No seer has read.
' But a moth,' you cry,
    ' Is a thing so small ! '
Ah, yes ; but why
    Should it suffer at all ?

Why should a sob
  For the vaguest smart
One moment throb
  Through the tiniest heart?
Why in the whole
  Wide universe
Should a single soul
  Feel that primal curse?
Not all the throes
  Of mightiest mind,
Nor the heaviest woes
  Of human kind,
Are of deeper weight
  In the riddle of things
Than that insect's fate
  With the mangled wings.

v

But if only I
  In my simple song
Could tell you the Why
  Of that one little wrong,
I could tell you more
  Than the deepest page
Of saintliest lore
  Or of wisest sage.

For never as yet
    In its wordy strife
Could Philosophy get
    At the import of life ;
And Theology's saws
    Have still to explain
The inscrutable cause
    For the being of pain.
So I somehow fear
    That in spite of both,
We are baffled here
    By this one singed moth.

IN BUSHEY PARK

THE crisp brown leaves break short which way we
  tread,
The golden faintly shiver overhead ;
  The lush Virginia creeper drapes the cottage
Aglow with mantling red.

Beneath, the beaded blades are spanned across
By countless dainty webs of silver floss ;
  While here and there a tiny sunlit brilliant
Twinkles among the moss.

Dear heart, since love first shaped our happier lot,
Some gleams of beauty lurk in every spot
  To flood my soul with that divine emotion
I once so vainly sought.

I found it not where solemn Alps and grey
Draw purple glories from the newborn day ;
  Nor where huge sombre pines loom overhanging
Niagara's rainbow spray ;

Nor in loud psalms whose palpitating strain
Thrills the vast dome of Buonarotti's fane;
 On canvas quick with Sandro's earnest passion,
Or Titian's statelier vein.

This mellow autumn morning makes me wise;
Within ourselves the spring of beauty lies;
 In thy true tender heart I read the secret,
In thy deep tender eyes.

ANIMALCULAR THEOLOGY

My dear Le Gallienne,
                        I, like you,
A dapper animalcule knew:
A philosophic monad he,
With most succinct theology.
While star on star aloft was hurled,
He crept, with us, on one small world:
About him, secular space lay filled
With myriad orbs that seethed and thrilled.
Vast forces, boundless energies,
Incalculable infinities,
Loomed awesome every starry night
Upon my animalcule's sight.
Eternities, within, without,
Steeped all my soul in reverent doubt.
I strove to read the Why and How
Of mystic æons, Then and Now:
I strained my eyes to penetrate
The ultimate atom, uncreate:

I heard the flutter of strange wings,
The infinitesimal pulse of things :
I watched the lurid whirlwinds veer
And eddy down the photosphere :
I pierced through æther to young stars
That blazed in fiery avatars :
With reeling brain I gazed and yearned
To know by what strange power they burned.
Amazed, to me our monad turned.
'What, don't you see how all was wrought ?'
He cried with smug face undistraught.
'A bigger monad, just like us,
Through primal chaos waving, thus,
One formless hand, bade all things be ;
And lo ! the sky, the land, the sea,
The stars, the worlds, and you, and me !'
'My friend,' quoth I, 'that surely seems
A vain conceit of monad dreams,
Too cramped to mirror such great themes :
For why should mites that creep and crawl
On one wee planet of them all
Believe their petty souls rehearse
The drama of the universe ?
Why fancy nature's cosmic plan
Modelled on monad or on man ?
Why dream such pygmy brains as these
Can grapple with immensities ?
Why make our narrow souls the die
To mould a congruous godhead by,

And deem the sum of things created
By one vast monad animated ?
Show me at least some proof, I urge,
Of your amœboid demiurge.'
'What ! ask for proof !' he cried aghast.
' Then has it come to this at last ?
Do miscreant mortals dare to flout,
In impious protozoan doubt
(Since men and monads grow so coxy),
Amœbamorphic orthodoxy ?
You scorn the wisdom of our sires,
Who took no heed of yon dim fires.
The ancient monads of our race
Were quite convinced that time and
    space,
With mind and matter, light and shade, ⎫
All eye hath seen or hand hath weighed, ⎬
One archetypal Monad made. ⎭
Not theirs to mete the eddying sun ;
To plumb the paths where comets run ;
To gauge the swift ethereal wave ;
To fathom night's abysmal cave.
Not theirs with studious eye to scan
The long-drawn birth of world or man.
For well they knew the whole was planned ⎫
(On lines that monads understand) ⎬
By one divine amœban hand. ⎭
If you refuse their creed to swallow,
I hold you flippant, pert, and shallow.

Fie on such heresy and schism !
'Tis sure the rankest atheism ! '
   I let him say his petulant say ;
Then, gently smiling, turned away,
To pit against his hasty guess
The overwhelming consciousness
Of man's and monad's littleness ;
Against his petty self-wrought Pope,
Micrometer and telescope ;
Against his dead ancestral lore,
Yon starry wastes my eyes explore ;
Against his crude divine afflatus,
This spectroscopic apparatus :
Secure that who would read the whole
Must scan it first from pole to pole,
And not expect at once to find
All worlds the mirror of his mind.

TO HERBERT SPENCER

DEEPEST and mightiest of our later seers,
   Spencer, whose piercing glance descried afar
Down fathomless rifts of dead unnumbered years
   The effulgent waste drift into sun or star,
And through vast wilds of elemental strife
Tracked out the first faint steps of yet unconscious
     life :

Thy hand has led us through the pathless maze,
   Chaotic sights and sounds that throng the brain,
Traced every strand along its tangled ways,
   And woven anew the many-coloured skein ;
Linked fact to fact in adamantine laws,
And shown through minds and worlds the unity of
     cause.

Ere thou hadst read the universal plan
   Our life was unto us a thing alone :
On this side nature stood, on that side man,
   Irreconcilable, as twain, not one :
Thy voice first told us man was nature's child,
And in one common law proclaimed them recon-
     ciled.

No partial system could suffice for thee,
   Whose eye has scanned the glittering fields of
      space,
Gazed through the æons on the fiery sea,
   And caught faint gleams of that ineffable face
Which, clad with earth and heaven and souls of men,
Hides its mysterious shape for ever from our ken.

As insect masons in some coral shoal,
   Piling the future mountain toward the sky,
Frame each his cell, unconscious of the whole,
   Live each his little life, and toil, and die ;
So we, the lesser workers in thy field,
Pile each the tiny heap our narrower range can yield.

But like some mighty architect, thy mind
   Works up the rock those lesser builders frame,
With conscious end and purpose clear defined,
   In arch and column, toward a single aim,
Till joining part to part thy broader soul
Rears high a stately fane, a grand harmonious whole.

Not without honour is the prophet's name,
   Save with his country and his kin in time ;
But after years shall noise abroad thy fame,
   Above all other fame in prose or rhyme :
For praise is his who builds for his own age,
But he who builds for Time must look to Time for
   wage.

Yet though thy purer spirit scorns to heed
   The vulgar guerdon of a brief renown,
Some little meed, at least, some little meed,
   Our age may add to thy more lasting crown.
Accept an unknown singer's thanks for light
Cast on the dim abyss that bounds our narrow sight.

1789-1848—1870

THE song of nations.   Sing and clap your hands :
Burst into blossom, all ye barren lands :
  She comes, to break the linkèd chains asunder,
And snap in twain the adamantine bands.

She came before.   Her cruel face and fair
Smote all our breasts with infinite despair :
  She passed.   The brightness of her lurid beauty
Was fiercer than our dazzled eyes could bear.

She came again.   In milder mien she came,
With fruits and flowers crowned, but still the same.
  One lurid day crushed down her risen splendour ;
She passed in murky clouds of smoke and flame.

Once more, she comes.   Surely our hearts are tried,
And every lesser passion cast aside :
  Shall she not dwell among us now for ever,
Our one and only love, our deathless bride ?

  (*Paris*, 1871.)

PISGAH

On the Moabite mount we stand,
  As stood the prophet of yore,
Looking down on the promised land
  That stretches before ;
A bountiful land that flows
  With milk and honey and wine,
And rich with the wealth that glows
  On olive and vine.

Through the wilderness of tears,
  Through a desert of thirsty sand,
We have journeyed these many years
  Toward the promised land.
Behind us the ages o'erpast
  Lie wrapped in a cloudy sheet,
But the promised land at last
  Smiles at our feet.

Blest above all that have been
  In the ages of old, are we,
For our eyes have dimly seen
  What their eyes shall see

D

Upon whom, in the fulness of light,
   Shall the sun of to-morrow be born,
To scatter the shades of the night
   With the arrows of morn.

Curst above all that have been
   And in all the ages shall be,
For the glory our eyes have seen
   Cursèd are we :
For we know the glory to come,
   The joy, and the light, and the love ;
But we know that our lips will be dumb
   Ere the slow years move.

Deep in the valley below
   We see the young men and maids,
Afar from the midday glow,
   In the sycamore shades ;
And the foot of the dancer trips
   In the dell of the coming years,
And the murmur of laughing lips
   Falls soft on our ears.

But softer and sweeter still
   True love is there to behold ;
And none may fetter his will
   With law or with gold :

And none may sully his wings
  With the deadly taint of lust,
But freest of all free things
  He soars from the dust.

Yet we have no share in the soil
  Whereto we have led our heirs;
We have borne the brunt of the toil,
  But the fruit is theirs.
For the vineyards are goodly and wide
  And more than a man may count,
But our grave shall be on the side
  Of the Moabite mount.

PESSIMIST

How dreamily the minutes pass
  As hand in hand we sit together
Here on this greener knoll of grass,
An islet in the waving mass
  Of purple heather.

How vague life's happiest moments seem,
  How keen and sharp and clear its sternest;
For joy is like a fitful gleam
Discerned through shadowy mists of dream :
  But pain alone is earnest.

Then let me steal one other kiss,
  Since earth is not so rich in treasure,
That you and I can lightly miss
A single poignant thrill of this
  Its deepest pleasure.

À BAS LA BOURGEOISIE

A PSALM OF THE COMMUNE

ONE race of ruthless spoil our fathers scattered
  When thro' the angry land a frantic nation
Rose in tumultuous mass and fiercely shattered
  The iron fetters of its degradation.

Their pitiless blood, rolled without touch of pity,
  In that first flush of freedom's wild commotion,
Down Rhône and Loire, from many a frenzied
    city,
  Encarnadined the purple breast of ocean.

Their stately homes stand empty and forsaken ;
  But in their stead a younger brood has risen,
Who on the nation's neck still sit unshaken,
  And make our sunny land a groaning prison.

Who piled a newer fane aloft to heaven
  Above the smoking shards of old oppression,
In whose unholy precinct, unforgiven,
  Still lurks the bastard brood of dead transgression.

Who doomed our men and maids to toilsome labour,
   In sunless sheds, like herds of driven cattle ;
Who picked our stalwart sons for sword or sabre,
   And drained the people's veins in useless battle.

Whose gilded pride rolled in voluptuous leisure
   Through fairest streets that banded toil could
     fashion :
Who piled them lofty halls of feverish pleasure
   To drown remorseful thought in fitful passion.

Whose foul hands soiled our wells of purest waters :
   Whose cruel arms in merciless embraces
Made harlots of the dearest of our daughters
   And scathed with eaten scars our fairest faces.

Who spared no holiest hope that heart can cherish,
   But chose our choicest maiden blood to slaken
Their thirsty lust, and left alone to perish
    The weary souls whose sweets their soul had
     taken.

Rise, Paris, rise, and like ten thousand devils
    Shake from thy breast these sons of godless
     barter ;
Feed with the relics of their sumptuous revels
    The famished mouths of Belleville and Mont-
     martre.

Glut in a sudden flood of vengeful madness
   The lifelong hunger of thy festering malice,
Whose hoarded hate is turned to fiendish gladness
   In one deep draught at that ensanguined chalice.

Small matter though thy blood with theirs must
   mingle,
   And though thy children's wailing drown their
   dirges :
Take sevenfold vengeance till thy shoulders tingle
   Beneath the frantic fury of thy scourges.

Close with thy spoilers in a deadly grapple :
   Wreak on their mitred priests thy angry warrant :
Hurl from their bases column, tower, and chapel :
   Rain on their palace roofs a fiery torrent :

Wrap in a robe of flame each spot where lingers
   The proud memorial of thy ancient story :
Clutch thy own throat with suicidal fingers,
   And perish mid the ruins of thy glory.

   (*Paris*, 1871.)

GAMBETTA

(A FALSIFIED PROPHECY)

November 1872

ONCE more she sits upon her ancient throne,
 The fair Republic of our steadfast vows ;
 A Phrygian bonnet binds her ivory brows,
About her neck her knotted hair is blown :
 A hundred cities nestle in her lap,
  Girt round their stately locks with mural
   crowns ;
 The folds of her imperial robe enwrap
  A thousand lesser towns.

But by her side in crownless state sits one
 Who in her darkest days with noble trust
 Raised up her fallen beauty from the dust,
And battled in her cause, her eldest son :
 Faithful alone through many a faithless hour,
  And proved by stern adversity of old ;
 Tried in the fiery crucible of power,
  And found of truest gold.

When on her neck the despot's heel was pressed,
  His eloquent voice alone rang loud and free
  To raise the trumpet cry of liberty
And speed her watchword on from east to west :
  And when, like some fierce whirlwind, through
    the land
    The wrathful Teuton swept, he only dared
  To hope and act when every heart and hand,
    But his alone, despaired.

A poet's scorn for all the ill that is ;
  A prophet's yearning for the distant weal ;
  A fervent tongue ; a heart of fiery zeal
Tempered with fine discretion, these are his :
  The earliest herald of that dawning day,
    When plans of weighty counsel shall arrange
  The younger world, while haste and slow
    delay
    Give place to gentle change.

He first among our chiefs had skill to wrench
  The iron pike from Revolution's hand,
  Pluck from her furious clutch the blazing brand,
And wrest the angry axe her fingers clench :
  His was the task to raise our slighted laws
    Without the murderous arm of anarchy,
  Winning at one bold stroke for freedom's cause
    A bloodless victory.

And now, when all our land is calm once more,
　　Like some fierce Ætna lulled a while to rest,
　　The fiery waves within whose torrent breast
Surge up to flood afresh the Rhenish shore ;
　　By timid friends and open foes begirt,
　　　　We find in him alone of all our men
　　One man too earnest-minded to desert
　　　　One brother citizen.

He still shall guide us toward the distant goal,
　　Calm with unerring tact our weak alarms,
　　Train all our youth in skill of manly arms,
And knit our sires in unity of soul,
　　Till bursting iron bars and gates of brass
　　　　Our own Republic stretch her arm again
　　To raise the weeping daughters of Alsace,
　　　　And lead thee home, Lorraine.

A VINDICATION

' Let him, the wiser man who springs
  Hereafter, up from childhood shape
  His action like the greater ape,
But I was born to other things.'

In Memoriam, cxx.

Ah, happy you who know your birth
Has loftier origin than earth :
I would not quench that generous fire,
But rather silently admire :
Yet if another, less in luck,
Amid his random thoughts has struck
Some clue which leads him on to think
Mankind is but the latest link
In being's endless, widening chain
Through higher types and higher again :
If, after months of patient thought,
His wavering mind is slowly brought
To grasp a simpler, humbler creed,
And deem himself an ape indeed ;

Then, having judged the notion true,
What should an ape of spirit do
But manfully resign his dream,
And take his rank in nature's scheme ?
   Nor need he, yet, behind him cast
The gathered greatness of the past.
He well may nurse each nobler thrill,
Each holier deed, each purer will.
Since earlier apes have raised their race
So high above its former place,
Why may not he as well aspire
To raise his race some places higher ?
To add an atom to the store
Of wisdom heaped by apes before ;
To feel within his hungry breast
Some goading spur of grand unrest,
Some glorious aim, in impulse rife,
That urges on to fuller life,
Nor leaves to rust in dull content
The powers a million ages lent.
   And surely such an ape as this
May live a life not much amiss ;
May love the right, eschew the wrong ;
Defend the weaker from the strong ;
Teach other after apes to be
Nobler and better far than he ;
In spite of calumny and scorn,
Mould younger ages yet unborn

To loftier thoughts and loftier still,
Beyond all human hope or will ;
Yet act, himself, his little part
On Nature's stage, with all his heart,
And show that even an ape may be
A credit to his ancestry.

IN THE NIGHT WATCHES

(INTRODUCTION TO A GROUP OF POEMS STILL
MOSTLY UNPUBLISHED)

SERVANT, awake and arise, for the people have slept
    overlong :
  Sing with the tongue that I bid thee a new and
    unlovable lay :
Sing of a pitiless race, and the blight of a terrible
    wrong,
  Ancient as infinite ages, and young as the morn
    of to-day.

Sing of the maiden thy sister, whom men thy
    brothers have sold,
  Cast on the merciless world, on the tide of the
    ravening years :
Bought with a price in the market, and paid with
    dishonour and gold ;
  Courted and loved and betrayed, and deserted to
    desolate tears.

Master, I pray thee, forbear ; for some other is
    fitter than I,
  Louder and clearer of tone to declare what thou
    wilt to the earth.
Mine is a fledgling of song, and its pinions are feeble
    to fly :
  Let me but listen in peace to the minstrels of
    love and of mirth.

May I not lie in the garden where singers before
    me have lain,
  Set to the sun and the summer, the edge of a
    flowery slope,
Far from the chills of the north and the whisper of
    sorrow or pain,
  Flooded with violet's odour and perfume of helio-
    trope ?

May I not nourish my fancy with visions of rap-
    turous bliss,
  Resonant echoes of Eden and phantoms of
    shadowy air ?
May I not sing of the sweetness and cover the
    sting of a kiss ?
  Tell of the honey of passion, and bury the gall
    of despair ?

Nay, for I bid thee arise with a sword in thy hand
      for a pen :
   Sharp be thy mouth as thou singest, and bitter
      the song thou shalt sing,
Weird with the wailing of women and cruel
      caresses of men.
   Others may tell of the honey of passion, but
      thou of the sting.

Hast thou not heard me of old in the feverish
      watches of night,
   Tossing awake on thy bed, how I whispered
      my word in thy ear ?
Have I not thundered it forth in the street in the
      fulness of light,
   Drowning the clamorous din of the city, and
      wilt thou not hear ?

Now, as I bid thee, arise on the timorous wings
      of thy song,
   Feeble and callow, but stayed by the might of
      the right for a stay :
Sing of a pitiless race and the blast of a terrible
      wrong,
   Poisonous, fiery, venomous.
                     Master, I hear and obey.

PASSIFLORA SANGUINEA

ALOOF she stood beneath the pallid glare
  That flashed and flickered through that garish
    bower ;
She wore a mystic symbol in her hair—
  A crimson passion-flower !

What wayward chance allotted unaware
  So apt an emblem of the years that lower
Above her fateful head, and twisted there
  That crimson passion-flower ?

Ah, innocent face, the blossom that you bear
  Fades in the amorous compass of an hour :
Red stains of martyred blood have flecked so fair
  Your crimson passion-flower ?

Some Judas kiss betrayed you to despair ;
  Dead thorns and cankered nails shall be your
    dower :
And with your own blood's price you bought and
    wear
  That crimson passion-flower.

E

MYLITTA

AMID the fleeting things whose changes drape
With ever-varying garb God's hidden shape,
    One form unchanged drifts down the eternal
    channel
Of pitiless years, that mortal hearts escape.

All else that earthly breathes is born and dies ;
Old generations fade, new faiths arise ;
    The empires pass away, the ages perish ;
But She lives on, a deathless sacrifice.

On her is laid the chastisement of all ;
On her our agonies and anguish fall ;
    For man's iniquity and woman's virtue
She bears the brand and drains the cup of gall.

Crowned with the thorns that lash our sin and
        pride,
Scourged all day long, and nightly crucified,
    Stricken and smitten for the world's trans-
    gression,
She shields the spotless maid and stainless bride.

Not for her sins her comely form is marred,
Her fair brow seared and her bruised shoulders
    scarred ;
  Wounded for all, she reaps but scorn and loathing
From those her lifelong pangs and travail guard.

Have none warm hearts, to share her hopes and
    fears ?
Chaste lips, to kiss away her scalding tears ?
  My sister, feed my mouth with gall and honey
That I may match my music with thy years :

Gall, from the bitter depths of thy disgrace ;
Honey, from the sweetness of thy martyred face :
  Gall, that my words may bite and sting and
    wither ;
Honey, to touch some lingering spot of grace.

For I have known the burden of thy groans ;
For I have felt, at sound of thy soft tones,
  The fitful love that melts to deathless pity,
The short desire that long remorse atones.

First Aphrodite lured me to thy shrine ;
I saw and loved that sweet strange form of thine,
  The smooth bared breast, the naked limbs and
    lissom,
The fair, pale cheek, the bright eye fired with wine.

But while my free gaze wandered its full range,
On face and form there fell some blighting change;
   The smooth bared breast grew lean, the lithe
      limbs listless,
The fair cheek wan, the bright eye glazed and
      strange.

Then all the heated fancy of my youth
Cooled at the solemn sight of that dread truth,
   And from the stifled fountain of my passion
Welled forth undying streams of infinite ruth.

Till, gently leaning o'er thy drooping head,
With lips that faltered as they spake, I said,
   'Make me the champion of thy blighted beauty,
That I may face this spell in thy dear stead.'

I spake and quivered: from thy dark grey eyes
Stole down twin glistening drops of glad surprise,
   As all the pent-up tenderness of woman
Flushed o'er thy cheek soft gleams of rosier guise.

Sweet sister, faithful to the inborn good,
Unsullied in thy gentle womanhood,
   Whose darkened days none else has learned to
      pity;
Whose scape-goat lot none else has understood:

What sin has blasted thee; what deadly crime
Has poisoned thy young life for endless time?
   The sin of love, the crime of trustful beauty,
The guileless innocence of thy maiden prime.

The lily nestling fairest in the glade
Is earliest plucked, and lightly left to fade;
   The deepest blushing rose is soonest gathered;
The truest trusting maiden first betrayed.

Yet is the compass of thy faith too great
For lifelong treacheries to desecrate.
   God, that a man should know these things, and
     scorn thee!
God, that a woman should know them not, and
     hate!

Oh brother men, oh maidens pure and fair,
And happier wives, made glad with matron care
   Of tiny pattering feet and baby laughter,
In your wide love has She alone no share?

Have not your hearts leapt forth when o'er the
     wave
Echoed the faint cry of some hapless slave?
   But see, to-day, our sister and our daughter
Sinks at our door, and none will heed or save.

Ah yet, be loth too lightly to despise
One that was precious in His tender eyes
    Who came to seek and save the lost and erring;
Whose voice still speaks: Go thou and do like-
    wise.

Bind up her wounds; pour in them oil and wine;
Wipe from her brimming eyes the dim hot brine;
    Hold to her fainting lips one cup of water:
The Master's little ones are kin of thine.

And if there be among the sons of men
Hearts that would scorn even Christ's own Mag-
    dalen,
    Then let them keep their saintly souls unsullied:
But we must do our Father's work.   Amen.

FORGET-ME-NOT

Her soft white hand lay tremulous, clasped in his;
    Her soft grey eye with pearly dew was wet :
He said, ' Though all things else, yet never this
    Will I forget.'

He went his way, and seeking his own rest
    Forgot love's little tender, stifled sigh,
Forgot the upheaval of that throbbing breast
    Once clasped so nigh.

And bending o'er an unmarked, uncared grave,
    Too late for any penance save regret,
He said, ' The single sin God ne'er forgave
    Is, to forget.'

SUNDAY NIGHT AT MABILLE

(SECOND EMPIRE)

GOOD reader, let me preach one short half-hour :
I am no priest ; but this is Sunday night ;
And if I will, may I not pick a text
From squalid palimpsests laid open here,
To read a pensive sermon to myself,
And, if you will, to you ?
                              Yes, Sunday night,
And here we are at Mabille !   All the air
Dances with some droll tune of Offenbach's,
Whose quaint notes caper round our startled ears
Like frolic imps that skip fantastic reels.
Bright forms are flitting through the shady alleys,
Festooned above with labyrinthine growth ;
While from ten thousand jets of coloured flame
Stream floods of light that shame the pale white
     day.
It seems some vulgar fairyland, this Mabille,
All light and life and merriment : and yet
Our eyes, perchance, bedazzled with its glare,
Behold it steeped in crimson of its lamps,
Too roseate for the solemn thing it is.

But if we come to-morrow, when pale dawn
Lights with chill gleams of dank reality
The desolate walks and broken ends of glass
And dingy pasteboard walls, then shall we know
What manner of place this Mabille is.

                                                Even so

With those gay forms that flit through Mabille's
    paths
This Sunday night: poor souls, right fair they
    look,
With bloom of Ninon on each painted cheek ;
And easy seems their life to such as judge
By Sunday nights at Mabille.   But *we* know
(Who view their stories by stern light of day)
How white those faces show without the rouge,
How sunk those shrivelled cheeks, how dull those
    eyes,
How sad those weary lives.   Quick, here, at one,
Mimi, this tricksy blonde, whose own fair curls
Shine golden bright among the duller locks
Bought from some Norman head—as I can see
The fair fresh nature of the village maid
Shine bright amid the borrowed nonchalant air
Of these Parisian orgies.   Mimi here,
Who looks so pretty and piquante a coquette,
Who flings a cancan with such saucy grace,
Who decks her in such rainbow silks and laces,—
Mimi is dying of the foulest death
That poisons earth.

      I 'll light my cigarette,
And then we 'll sink on seats and watch the world,
And break a bottle of St. Peray.
          Of old
One told us, ' The dark places of the earth
Are full of wickedness.' I am no priest,
But I could read a sermon on that text
(' Dark places,' quoth the innocent Hebrew bard !)
Beneath the dazzling lights that flood Mabille
This Sunday night. Ay, ' full of wickedness,'
And fuller still of misery and pain.
The pulpit preacher, an we had him here,
Could spill cheap vials of wrath upon the heads
Of these poor blighted things that once were
  women :
But you and I, who know their desolate days
And dreary desolate nights—we who have seen
The white-faced corpses wasted to the bone,
Or laid in marble nakedness at the Morgue
(A sight for whoso dare to stand and gaze)—
We two, who know they find their hell on earth,
Have little need to scare them with a hell
Hotter and redder still to follow this :
And little need to cry ' 'Ware sin ! ' to those
Who know not if indeed it be a sin
To be betrayed by poverty or man
To deepest depths of fathomless despair,
But know at least that shame and scorn and pain
Are bitter morsels.

And these men who chat
So gaily with them, men with lives made bright
By mothers' love and sisters', ay, perchance
(Who knows?) and sweethearts'; happy men and
    young,
Oh, can they deem that they, who would not crush
One shard-mailed creeping thing for very pity,
Are lightly bargaining for women's lives
And cheapening flesh and blood against champagne?
Good preacher, pour your choicest vial on these!
    Yet am I no ascetic: I can spend
My Sunday night at Mabille, and enjoy
My cigarette and bottle of St. Peray
As well as you, good reader: ay, and love
A pretty face; I said I was no priest.
But he who truly loves a pretty face
Finds sight of pretty faces wan with care,
And happy hearts made sick with hope deferred,
And death that slowly creeps and still delays,
The saddest sight that darkens human eyes.
    Why have I brought you then to see Mabille
This Sunday night? you ask.—To find my text
And point my sermon.   Here you have its gist.
—You tell me we must shut our eyes to all
That turns this gaudy Mabille to a hell,
If we would keep our wives and daughters pure.
So be it: I know not.   But if we must hold
So many hearts in anguish and despair,
So many lives that once were blithe and free

In tenfold slavery, to guard the rest
From some slight taint of ill ; then, staring round
At all the hapless forms that crowd Mabille,
And knowing all that we have seen and said,
And feeling all this life in need of change,
One question ever rises to my lips,
One question that I scarcely dare to breathe :—
If woman's virtue cost so much to keep,
Good friend, is woman's virtue worth the price ?

FORECAST AND FULFILMENT

She shall be tall and slight ; of swanlike mien ;
White brow, and melting tints upon her cheek ;
Dusk tresses where the nestling sunbeams spread
A liquid halo : but with haughty eyes
And chiselled features of a high-born maid,
Bearing an awesome presence where she treads.
Her dainty lips shall utter ringing words,
High solemn talk of chastened love, and themes
That rouse a nobler swelling in the pulse,
Or quicken every nerve to quiver and leap :
A very queen of women, to rule my life
With royal dignity and royal grace.
Our souls shall dwell above the thoughts of men,
In Fancy's high demesne ; therein shall we
The livelong summer noontide weave sweet
    dreams,
In some dim alcove, where the crimson light
Through deep-embrasured oriels flickers down
To paint the oaken panels : happy dreams,
In unison of heart, where each may bare

The spirit's inmost yearning, and in turn
Read its true image in a kindred soul.
No hunger there, nor wish insatiate,
But every chord shall wake a meet response.
So she and I, a single twinfold life,
Shall tread this dull earth with a mellow light
Shed round our happier heads; and, all absorbed
Each in the other, merge our several selves,
Clasped in one long embrace of wedded souls.

.   .   .   .   .   .

So in fantastic mood I idly muse
Beneath the budding chestnuts on the marge,
What time the wan leaves burst their dusky
        sheaths,
And herald May.   Beside, the lazy boats
Glide down the crawling stream with regular dip,
Plashing their mimic ripplets in the flags;
And all around the lilacs' fragrant mist
Hangs on the stagnant air.   But Love stands by,
Smiling to watch the visions that I paint,
And, while my veins beat full with spring and
        youth,
Works out his own sweet will, his own sweet way.

.   .   .   .   .   .

Small is she, like some jewel; but passing fair;
Eyes soft and blue, wherein does laughter lurk,
And dimpled cheeks and chin.   Two smiling lips,
Pout forth sweet, saucy words of petulant love;

And in my hand lies clasped a tiny hand,
So small, 'tis almost pity 'tis so small.
No queen of women she, but my true wife,
Who treads on solid earth, and breathes, and loves,
Even as others breathe and love.   Her themes
No lofty phantasies or dreamy shadows,
But winsome words that cheer the wearied heart,
And happy plans for summer afternoon,
Or winter pastime : while her merry eyes
Flash laughter into mine, or, brimmed with mist,
Cast matron shadows on the sobered face,
Yet woo my lips to check the gathering drop.
Around my heart she twines her clinging arms,
And loves, and knows not why, nor doubts for
    love ;
But only knows the world is great and cold,
And turns, and nestles closer by my side,
Secure in supreme faith.   But on her lap,
More sweet than all, so love could find more
    sweet,
A tiny maiden sleeps, and sleeping smiles :
A waxen lily bud, with cheek and chin,
Dimple for dimple : and we watch and smile,
And catch the mutual sunbeams in our eyes ;
And two hearts breathe one prayer to loving
    Heaven,
For Love's sweet will is wrought his own sweet
    way.

www.ingramcontent.com/pod-product-compliance
Lightning Source LLC
Chambersburg PA
CBHW032350020726
47499CB00008B/2691